JavaScript Testing with Jasmine

Evan Hahn

O'REILLY®

Beijing · Cambridge · Farnham · Köln · Sebastopol · Tokyo

JavaScript Testing with Jasmine

by Evan Hahn

Printed in the United States of America.

Published by O'Reilly Media, Inc., 1005 Gravenstein Highway North, Sebastopol, CA 95472.

O'Reilly books may be purchased for educational, business, or sales promotional use. Online editions are also available for most titles (*http://my.safaribooksonline.com*). For more information, contact our corporate/institutional sales department: 800-998-9938 or *corporate@oreilly.com*.

Editor: Mary Treseler	**Cover Designer:** Karen Montgomery
Production Editor: Marisa LaFleur	**Interior Designer:** David Futato
Proofreader: Rachel Monaghan	**Illustrator:** Rebecca Demarest

March 2013:   First Edition

Revision History for the First Edition:

2013-03-22:   First release

See *http://oreilly.com/catalog/errata.csp?isbn=9781449356378* for release details.

ISBN: 978-1-449-35637-8

[LSI]

Table of Contents

Preface

All programmers want their code to work the way they intended. Jasmine, a popular testing framework for the JavaScript programming language, allows you to achieve that goal. Through coded specifications, Jasmine helps make your JavaScript work exactly how it's supposed to. In this book, we'll explore Jasmine in detail, from its basic concepts to its advanced features.

This book aims to explain the concepts of testing and test-driven development, as well as why they're useful. It then aims to dive into Jasmine and explain how it can help programmers test their JavaScript code. By the end of this book, I aim to give readers an understanding of Jasmine's concepts and syntax.

Who Should Read This Book

This book is intended for programmers who are familiar with some more advanced JavaScript features, such as closures and callbacks, and who have a general understanding of JavaScript's prototype system. If you are interested in learning how to write reliable JavaScript code, this is the book for you.

Jasmine is useful when building a maintainable and scalable JavaScript application, either in a browser or on a server. It can help ensure that a browser's client-side data models are performing properly, or that a server is correctly serving pages.

Jasmine is also useful for building reliable JavaScript libraries. It can help ensure that the exposed API of your library matches what you intend it to match.

Conventions Used in This Book

The following typographical conventions are used in this book:

Italic

Indicates new terms, URLs, email addresses, filenames, and file extensions.

`Constant width`

> Used for program listings, as well as within paragraphs to refer to program elements such as variable or function names, databases, data types, environment variables, statements, and keywords.

 This icon signifies a tip, suggestion, or general note.

Using Code Examples

This book is here to help you get your job done. In general, if this book includes code examples, you may use the code in this book in your programs and documentation. You do not need to contact us for permission unless you're reproducing a significant portion of the code. For example, writing a program that uses several chunks of code from this book does not require permission. Selling or distributing a CD-ROM of examples from O'Reilly books does require permission. Answering a question by citing this book and quoting example code does not require permission. Incorporating a significant amount of example code from this book into your product's documentation does require permission.

We appreciate, but do not require, attribution. An attribution usually includes the title, author, publisher, and ISBN. For example: "*JavaScript Testing with Jasmine* by Evan Hahn (O'Reilly). Copyright 2013 Evan Hahn, 978-1-4493-5637-8."

If you feel your use of code examples falls outside fair use or the permission given above, feel free to contact us at *permissions@oreilly.com*.

Safari® Books Online

 *Safari Books Online* is an on-demand digital library that delivers expert content in both book and video form from the world's leading authors in technology and business.

Technology professionals, software developers, web designers, and business and creative professionals use Safari Books Online as their primary resource for research, problem solving, learning, and certification training.

Safari Books Online offers a range of product mixes and pricing programs for organizations, government agencies, and individuals. Subscribers have access to thousands of books, training videos, and prepublication manuscripts in one fully searchable database from publishers like O'Reilly Media, Prentice Hall Professional, Addison-Wesley Professional, Microsoft Press, Sams, Que, Peachpit Press, Focal Press, Cisco Press, John

Wiley & Sons, Syngress, Morgan Kaufmann, IBM Redbooks, Packt, Adobe Press, FT Press, Apress, Manning, New Riders, McGraw-Hill, Jones & Bartlett, Course Technology, and dozens more. For more information about Safari Books Online, please visit us online.

How to Contact Us

Please address comments and questions concerning this book to the publisher:

O'Reilly Media, Inc.
1005 Gravenstein Highway North
Sebastopol, CA 95472
800-998-9938 (in the United States or Canada)
707-829-0515 (international or local)
707-829-0104 (fax)

We have a web page for this book, where we list errata, examples, and any additional information. You can access this page at *http://oreil.ly/JS_Jasmine*.

To comment or ask technical questions about this book, send email to *bookquestions@oreilly.com*.

For more information about our books, courses, conferences, and news, see our website at *http://www.oreilly.com*.

Find us on Facebook: *http://facebook.com/oreilly*

Follow us on Twitter: *http://twitter.com/oreillymedia*

Watch us on YouTube: *http://www.youtube.com/oreillymedia*

Acknowledgments

Thanks to RockMelt for asking me to learn Jasmine.

Thanks to Pivotal Labs for creating Jasmine.

Thanks to my parents for their constant support.

CHAPTER 1

Intro to Testing

What Is Software Testing?

In short, you can test software against a specification.

Let's say you're writing a simple calculator that just does addition. Before you even start, think about how it should behave. It should be able to add positive integers. It should be able to add negative integers. It should be able to add decimal numbers, not just integers. You can think of many different ways that your calculator needs to work.

Before you've written any of the code, you know how you want it to behave. You have a *specification* for its behavior.

You can write these specifications in code. You'd say, "OK, it should work this way." You'd make tests that added 1 and 1, 2 and 2, −1 and 5, −1.2 and 6.8, 0 and 0, and so on. When you run these tests, you'll either get a success (it works according to the specification) or a failure (it doesn't). If you ran all of your tests and saw success for each, then you can be pretty sure that your calculator works. If you ran these tests and saw some failures, then you know that your calculator doesn't work.

That's software testing in a nutshell. You're testing your code against a specification. There are many tools (Jasmine among them) that help you automate these software tests.

It's important to know that it's difficult (and often impossible) to write tests for *every* case. In the calculator example, there are an infinite number of possible combinations. When testing, you should try to cover every reasonable case by testing a number of different groups (integers, negative numbers, mixes of the two, etc.). You should also identify boundary conditions (zeroes, for example) and edge cases, testing as many different scenarios as possible.

Why Is It Useful?

Testing is useful for a number of reasons.

First, these tests can evaluate a program's correctness after a change. Let's say all the tests are passing, and then I decide I want one of my functions to be faster. I can dive in, make some changes, and see that it is indeed faster. But if I run the tests again and see that some are failing, I quickly discover that my fix has broken some part of the code. Automated testing lets me see those errors before they happen in the "real world."

These tests can also function as good examples for other developers. If a developer is trying to figure out how to use some undocumented part of your code, a well-written test can help him see how that piece works.

Test-Driven Development

A relatively new software development technique is called *test-driven development*, or TDD. The process works like this:

1. Write test cases for a specific part of your code. In the calculator example, you'd write tests for adding positive numbers, negative numbers, integers, and so on. You haven't written the calculator yet, so all of these tests should fail!

2. Write your code to "fill in" the tests. Your code *only* serves to make all of your tests pass, and nothing more.

3. Once all of your tests pass, go back and clean up your code (this is called *refactoring*).

Test-driven development allows developers to think clearly about the specifications *before* their minds are clouded with the implementation details. It also ensures that tests are always written, which is always useful.

Behavior-Driven Development

With *behavior-driven development*, or BDD, you write specifications that are small and easy to read. There are basically two key parts of BDD:

1. Your tests must be small and test one thing. Instead of testing the entire application, you write *many* small tests. In the calculator example, you would write one test for each addition pair: one test for 0 + 0, one test for 1 + 1, one test for −5 + 6, one test for 6.2 + 1.2, and so on.

2. Your tests should be sentences. In the calculator example, sentences would look like "Calculator adds two positive integers." The testing framework that you use (Jasmine, in this book's case) should do this automatically for you.

These two tenets allow you to run your test suite and see *exactly* what's wrong at a glance. If you see a bunch of successes but one failure on "Calculator adds two negative numbers," you know where to look.

Dan North is credited with BDD's invention. He describes the system in more detail on his website (*http://dannorth.net/introducing-bdd/*).

So, enough about testing. What's Jasmine?

CHAPTER 2

Jasmine

What Is Jasmine?

Jasmine is a behavior-driven testing framework for JavaScript programming language. It's a bunch of tools that you can use to test JavaScript code.

As you learned in the previous chapter, you can test your code against specifications that you write. If your code should work in a certain way, Jasmine helps you express that intention in code.

(By the way: if you've played around with RSpec for testing Ruby, Jasmine will look suspiciously familiar.)

Getting Set Up with Jasmine

Start by downloading the latest standalone release of Jasmine (*http://bit.ly/ZAgJqg*). Unzip it.

 Throughout this book, we'll mostly be using browser-based Jasmine for various reasons. If you'd prefer a different environment (Node.js, Ruby/ Rails, or other environments), take a look at Chapter 7, or the Jasmine wiki (*https://github.com/pivotal/jasmine/wiki*). These instructions are for a browser-based environment.

When you open *SpecRunner.html* in a web browser, you'll see something like Figure 2-1.

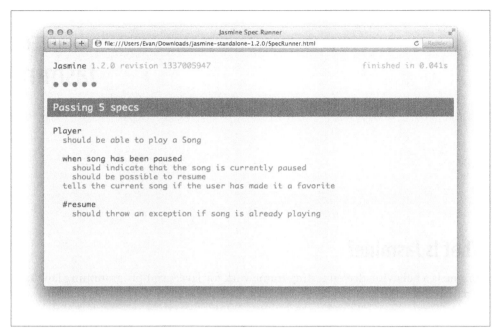

Figure 2-1. First time running Jasmine!

This file has run some example tests on some example code. It's testing a Player and a Song. Whenever you want to run the tests, you simply need to load/reload this page.

In the *src* directory, you'll see two things to be tested: a Player and a Song. The *spec* directory has tests for the Player. Taking a look inside the *spec* directory might help you understand Jasmine's syntax (though there's also this fine book to help with that).

You probably don't want to test this example code, so you should empty out the *spec* and *src* directories. When you change the filenames, you'll have to edit *SpecRunner.html* to point to the right files (there are comments that indicate what you should change). We'll go through how to do that next.

Testing Existing Code with describe, it, and expect

To learn Jasmine, let's write some example code and then test it with Jasmine.

An Example to Test

First, let's create a simple function and test its behavior. It'll say hello to the *entire world*. It could look something like this:

```
function helloWorld() {
    return "Hello world!";
}
```

You're pretty sure that this works, but you want to test it with Jasmine to see what it thinks. Start by saving this in the *src* directory as *hello.js*. Open up your *SpecRunner.html* file to include it:

```
<!-- put this code somewhere in the <head>... -->
<script type="text/javascript" src="src/hello.js"></script>
```

Note that the order doesn't matter—you can put the specs before or after the source files.

Jasmine Time!

Next is the Jasmine part. Get ready to get your money's worth for this book.

Make a file that includes the following code:

```
describe("Hello world", function() {
    it("says hello", function() {
        expect(helloWorld()).toEqual("Hello world!");
    });
});
```

describe("Hello world"... is what is called a *suite*. The name of the suite ("Hello world" in this case) typically defines a component of your application; this could be a class, a function, or maybe something else fun. This suite is called "Hello world"; it's a string of English, not code.

Inside of that *suite* (technically, inside of an anonymous function), is the it() block. This is called a *specification*, or a *spec* for short. It's a JavaScript function that says what some small piece of your component should do. It says it in plain English ("says hello") and in code. For each suite, you can have any number of specs for the tests you want to run.

In this case, you're testing if helloWorld() does indeed return "Hello world!". This check is called a *matcher*. Jasmine includes a number of predefined matchers, but you can also define your own (we'll get to that in Chapter 4). We expect the output of helloWorld() to equal (toEqual) the string "Hello world!".

Jasmine aims to read like English, so it's possible that you were able to intuit how this example worked just by looking at it. If not, don't worry!

Save that code as *hello.spec.js*, put it in the *spec* directory, and make sure that your spec runner knows about it:

```
<!-- put this code somewhere in the <head>... -->
<script type="text/javascript" src="spec/hello.spec.js"></script>
```

If you run this spec in the browser, you'll see the output shown in Figure 2-2.

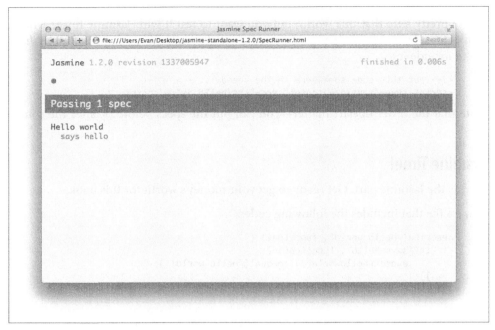

Figure 2-2. Hello world specs

Success!

Go into the helloWorld() function and make it say something other than "Hello world!". When you run the specs again, Jasmine will complain. That's what you want; Jasmine should tell you when you've done something you didn't intend to.

Matchers

In the previous example, you were checking to see if helloWorld() was indeed equal to "Hello world!". You used the function toEqual(), which—as noted earlier—is a *matcher*. This basically takes the argument to the expect function (which is hello World(), in this case) and checks to see if it satisfies some criterion in the matcher. In the preceding example, it checks if the argument is equal to something else.

But what if we wanted to expect it to contain the word "world," but we don't care what else is in there? We just want it to say "world." Easy peasy; we just need to use a different matcher: toContain. Have a look:

```
describe("Hello world", function() {
    it("says world", function() {
```

```
        expect(helloWorld()).toContain("world");
    });
});
```

Instead of expecting something to equal "Hello world!", I'm now just expecting it to *contain* "world." It even reads like English! There are a lot of bundled matchers, and you can even make your own. We'll learn how to do that in Chapter 4.

Writing the Tests First with Test-Driven Development

Jasmine can easily test existing code; you write the code first and test it second. Test-driven development is the opposite: you write the tests first, and then "fill in" the tests with code.

As an example, let's try using test-driven development (TDD) to make a "disemvoweler." A disemvoweler removes all vowels from a string (let's assume that the letter *y* isn't a vowel in this example, and that we're dealing with English). What does our disemvoweler do (i.e. what does the specification look like)?

- It should remove all lowercase vowels.
- It should remove all uppercase vowels.
- It shouldn't change empty strings.
- It shouldn't change strings with no vowels.

Now, let's think of some examples that would test the preceding specifications:

- Remove all lowercase vowels: "Hello world" should become "Hll wrld".
- Remove all uppercase vowels: "Artistic Eagle" should become "rtstc gl".
- Don't change empty strings: "" should stay "".
- Don't change strings with no vowels: "Mhmm" should stay "Mhmm".

Jasmine makes it easy to codify these specifications:

```
describe("Disemvoweler", function() {
    it("should remove all lowercase vowels", function() {
        expect(disemvowel("Hello world")).toEqual("Hll wrld");
    });
    it("should remove all uppercase vowels", function() {
        expect(disemvowel("Artistic Eagle")).toEqual("rtstc gl");
    });
    it("shouldn't change empty strings", function() {
        expect(disemvowel("")).toEqual("");
    });
    it("shouldn't change strings with no vowels", function() {
        expect(disemvowel("Mhmm")).toEqual("Mhmm");
```

```
    });
});
```

Save this code into *spec/DisemvowelSpec.js* and include it in *SpecRunner.html*:

```
<script type="text/javascript" src="spec/DisemvowelSpec.js"></script>
```

If you refresh the spec runner, you'll see what's shown in Figure 2-3.

Figure 2-3. Failing disemvoweler specs

All of your specs fail! This is expected—you haven't written any of the code yet, so Jasmine can't find any function called `disemvowel`. It's helpful to see your tests fail because you know you're protected against false positives this way. (If a test passed with no code written, something is wrong!)

Let's write a first version of our disemvoweler:

```
function disemvowel(str) {
    return str.replace(/a|e|i|o|u/g, "");
}
```

This code uses a regular expression to substitute any vowel with an empty string. Save this into *src/Disemvowel.js* and add that into the spec runner:

```
<script type="text/javascript" src="src/Disemvowel.js"></script>
```

Refresh the spec runner, and you should see something like Figure 2-4.

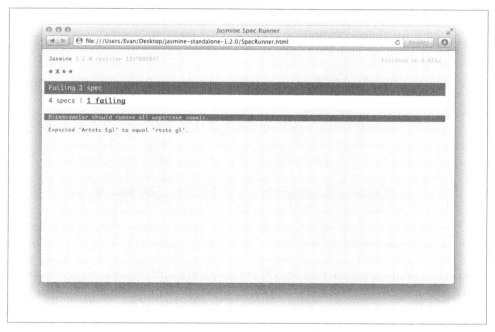

Figure 2-4. Only one disemvoweler spec failing!

Instead of all of the specs failing, only one is failing now. It looks like the disemvoweler isn't removing all the uppercase vowels. Jasmine helps us see where the problem is: our first version wouldn't remove *any* uppercase vowels. Let's add the case-insensitive flag (i) to our regular expression:

```
function disemvowel(str) {
    return str.replace(/a|e|i|o|u/gi, "");
}
```

Save that and rerun the spec runner. See Figure 2-5.

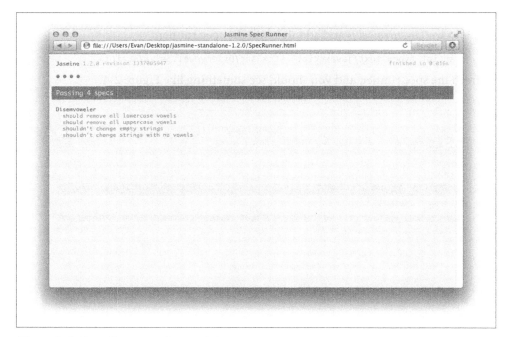

Figure 2-5. Our disemvoweler works!

It looks like our disemvoweler works! That's a simple example of how to write code using TDD: tests come first, implementation comes second.

CHAPTER 3

Writing Good Tests

So, now you know how to write tests with Jasmine. In theory, you could write an infinite number of tests for your code, testing weird conditions and more, but you don't have unlimited time on your hands. You have to write the correct specs for the job.

This is subjective; none of this is gospel by any means. These are simply my recommendations after having worked with Jasmine on a number of projects.

Cardinal Rule: When in Doubt, Test

If you're not sure whether or not to test something, it probably doesn't hurt to test it. If it would take you, as the developer, a long time to develop the spec, you might want to make sure you really need to build it. If it'd make Jasmine run slowly (perhaps it's doing a large computation), you might also want to reconsider. Usually, specs are pretty short and pretty speedy, so if you're not sure, make a spec!

Test Components

Test individual components of your code, rather than everything at once. For example, if you have a Calculator class, you don't want to test it like this:

```
describe("calculator addition", function() {
    it("can add, subtract, multiply, and divide positive integers",
        function() {
        var calc = new Calculator;
        expect(calc.add(2, 3)).toEqual(5);
        expect(calc.sub(8, 5)).toEqual(3);
        expect(calc.mult(4, 3)).toEqual(12);
        expect(calc.div(12, 4)).toEqual(3);
    });
});
```

That large spec should be split up into four different specs, because you're really testing four different parts. This is a step in the right direction:

```
describe("calculator addition", function() {
    var calc;
    beforeEach(function() {
        calc = new Calculator();
    });
    it("can add positive integers", function() {
        expect(calc.add(2, 3)).toEqual(5);
    });
    it("can subtract positive integers", function() {
        expect(calc.sub(8, 5)).toEqual(3);
    });
    it("can multiply positive integers", function() {
        expect(calc.mult(4, 3)).toEqual(12);
    });
    it("can divide positive integers", function() {
        expect(calc.div(12, 4)).toEqual(3);
    });
});
```

Each spec should test only one case or scenario at a time. In the previous example, if you had an error in your `mult` function, the spec would fail even if the other components worked perfectly. In this example, only one test will fail, and you'll be able to more quickly pinpoint that your multiplication is broken.

Black-Box Testing

When writing behavior-focused tests, you can imagine your software being a black box. You care only about the software's behavior, not what happens internally.

A simple example: if your `person` object has a function that includes a private method (not *technically* private, sorry) called `_generateHello`, it might look like this when calling `helloWorld`:

```
var person = {
    // Private method
    _generateHello: function() {
        return "hello";
    },
    // Public method
    helloWorld: function() {
        return this._generateHello() + " world";
    }
};
```

Because `_generateHello` is a private method, *you'd never test that in Jasmine.* You don't need to, because you don't care how it works. You just care how the public method works.

CHAPTER 4

Matchers in Depth

There are a lot of useful matchers that come with Jasmine. Later in this section, you'll also see how to build your own.

Equality: toEqual

Perhaps the simplest matcher in Jasmine is `toEqual`. It simply checks if two things are equal (and *not* necessarily the same exact object, as you'll see in Chapter 5).

The following `expect` functions will pass:

```
expect(true).toEqual(true);
expect([1, 2, 3]).toEqual([1, 2, 3]);
expect({}).toEqual({});
```

Here are some examples of `toEqual` that will fail:

```
expect(5).toEqual(12);
expect([1, 2, 3, 4]).toEqual([1, 2, 3]);
expect(true).toEqual(100);
```

Keep in mind that this is different from the `toBe` matcher. The subtle difference is noted next.

Identity: toBe

At first, the `toBe` matcher looks a lot like the `toEqual` matcher, but it's not exactly the same. `toBe` checks if two things are *the same object*, not just if they are equivalent.

Here's an example spec that illustrates the difference between `toEqual` and `toBe`:

```
var spot = { species: "Border Collie" };
var cosmo = { species: "Border Collie" };
expect(spot).toEqual(cosmo);  // success; equivalent
```

```
expect(spot).toBe(cosmo);    // failure; not the same object
expect(spot).toBe(spot);     // success; the same object
```

We see that, although spot and cosmo look really similar and are equal, *they aren't the same object*. Because of that, they evaluate as *equal*, not *the same*.

The same is also true for arrays:

```
var arr = [1, 2, 3];
expect(arr).toEqual([1, 2, 3]);   // success; equivalent
expect(arr).toBe([1, 2, 3]);      // failure; not the same array
```

You might notice that toBe works for primitives (numbers, Booleans, strings). This is because JavaScript's === operator evaluates primitives as the same entity. Using toBe is essentially using the === operator.

Use toEqual when checking the equivalence of primitive types, even if toBe will work. Using toBe might break your tests if you later decide to change a number to an array, for example.

For more about how this nuance works in JavaScript, see the video JavaScript Primitive Types vs Reference Types (*http://youtu.be/mh-hPzDfb_Q*).

Yes or No? toBeTruthy, toBeFalsy

To test if something evaluates to true, you use the toBeTruthy matcher:

```
expect(true).toBeTruthy();
expect(12).toBeTruthy();
expect({}).toBeTruthy();
```

Likewise, to test if something evaluates to false, you use toBeFalsy:

```
expect(false).toBeFalsy();
expect(null).toBeFalsy();
expect("").toBeFalsy();
```

Note that Jasmine's evaluation of truthy and falsy are identical to JavaScript's. This means that true is truthy, but so is "Hello world", or the number 12, or an object. It's useful to think of all the things that are falsy, and then everything else as truthy.

For reference, here's a list of things that are falsy in Jasmine (and in JavaScript, too):

- false
- 0
- ""
- undefined (note that the variable undefined isn't always undefined!)

- null

- NaN

If you haven't seen NaN before, it's a special number value that stands for *Not a Number*. It represents nonsensical number values like 0/0. It's also returned by some functions that return numbers (for example, parseInt("hello") returns NaN because it cannot properly parse a number).

If you want to make sure something is literally true or false and nothing else, use the toEqual matcher like so:

```
expect(myVariable).toEqual(true);
expect(myOtherVariable).toEqual(false);
```

Negate Other Matchers with not

It's frequently useful to reverse Jasmine's matchers to make sure that they aren't true. To do that, simply prefix things with .not:

```
expect(foo).not.toEqual(bar);
expect("Hello planet").not.toContain("world");
```

Check If an Element Is Present with toContain

Sometimes you want to verify that an element is a member of an array, *somewhere*. To do that, you can use the toContain matcher:

```
expect([1, 2, 3, 4]).toContain(3);
expect(["Penguin", "Turtle", "Pig", "Duck"]).toContain("Duck");
```

Note that toContain doesn't check if the array contains *the exact same object*, so the following example will succeed:

```
var dog = { name: "Fido" };
expect([
    { name: "Spike" },
    { name: "Fido" },
    { name: "Spot" }
]).toContain(dog);
```

The toContain matcher also works in strings, as we saw in the first example of this book:

```
expect("Hello world").toContain("world");
expect(favoriteCandy).not.toContain("Almond");
```

Is It Defined? toBeDefined, toBeUndefined

As with truthiness and falsiness, there are matchers to check if something is defined or undefined.

Before we start, let's briefly review JavaScript's notion of undefined and how it compares to null: when you declare a new variable with no value specified, its type is "undefined" (just like 123's type is "number"). In other languages, it might be null or nil. Not in JavaScript! There's a lot of confusion around this, but it doesn't directly apply to Jasmine.

For more background on undefined and how it works, check out Understanding Java-Script's "undefined" (*http://bit.ly/14XHBU3*).

Here are a few examples to demonstrate how these matchers work:

```
var somethingUndefined;
expect("Hello!").toBeDefined();                   // success
expect(null).toBeDefined();                        // success
expect(somethingUndefined).toBeDefined();          // failure

var somethingElseUndefined;
expect(somethingElseUndefined).toBeUndefined();    // success
expect(12).toBeUndefined();                        // failure
expect(null).toBeUndefined();                      // failure
```

It's worth noting that the variables you're checking have to be defined. The following code throws a ReferenceError and will fail:

```
it("tests toBeUndefined", function() {
  expect(someUndefinedVariable).toBeUndefined();
  // Throws a ReferenceError because someUndefinedVariable hasn't been declared.
});
```

Nullness: toBeNull

The toBeNull matcher is fairly straightforward. If you hadn't guessed by now, it checks if something is null:

```
expect(null).toBeNull();              // success
expect(false).toBeNull();             // failure
expect(somethingUndefined).toBeNull(); // failure
```

Fairly simple!

Is It NaN? toBeNaN

Like toBeNull, toBeNaN checks if something is NaN:

```
expect(5).not.toBeNaN();             // success
expect(0 / 0).toBeNaN();             // success
expect(parseInt("hello")).toBeNaN(); // success
```

This is different from JavaScript's built-in isNaN function. The built-in isNaN will return true for many nonnumber types, such as nonnumeric strings, objects, and arrays. Jasmine's will be positive only if it's the NaN value.

Comparators: toBeGreaterThan, toBeLessThan

The toBeGreaterThan and toBeLessThan matchers check if something is greater than or less than something else. All of these will pass:

```
expect(8).toBeGreaterThan(5);
expect(5).toBeLessThan(12);
expect("a").toBeLessThan("z"); // Notice that it works for strings too!
```

Not too difficult!

Nearness: toBeCloseTo

toBeCloseTo allows you to check if a number is close to another number, given a certain amount of decimal precision as the second argument.

If you want to make sure that a variable is close to 12.3 within one decimal point, you'd code it like this:

```
expect(12.34).toBeCloseTo(12.3, 1); // success
```

If you want it to be the same within two decimal points, you'd change the 1 to a 2. This spec will fail, though—they differ at the second decimal digit:

```
expect(12.34).toBeCloseTo(12.3, 2); // failure
```

In this case, *any* second argument over 2 will fail, so the following will fail as well:

```
expect(12.34).toBeCloseTo(12.3, 3); // failure
expect(12.34).toBeCloseTo(12.3, 4); // failure
expect(12.34).toBeCloseTo(12.3, 5); // failure
// and so on...
```

Setting the second argument to 0 effectively rounds the numbers to integers:

```
expect(12.3456789).toBeCloseTo(12, 0);     // success
expect(500).toBeCloseTo(500.087315, 0);    // success
expect(500.087315).toBeCloseTo(500, 0);    // success
```

I find toBeCloseTo a little confusing and limiting. In "Custom Matchers" on page 20, we'll make a matcher that aims to improve it.

Using toMatch with Regular Expressions

toMatch checks if something is matched, given a regular expression. It can be passed as a regular expression *or* a string, which is then parsed as a regular expression. All of the following will succeed:

```
expect("foo bar").toMatch(/bar/);
expect("horse_ebooks.jpg").toMatch(/\w+.(jpg|gif|png|svg)/i);
expect("jasmine@example.com").toMatch("\w+@\w+\.\w+");
```

For more on regular expressions in JavaScript, check out this very helpful article (*http:// mzl.la/WnQ5Dn*) on the Mozilla Developer Network. (Note that these regular expression examples aren't as thorough as they could be—a better email regular expression is very long!)

Checking If a Function Throws an Error with toThrow

toThrow lets you express, "Hey, I expect this function to throw an error":

```
var throwMeAnError = function() {
    throw new Error();
};
expect(throwMeAnError).toThrow();
```

You can use this with anonymous functions too, which can be more useful. For example, let's say there's a function that should throw an exception with bad input, like so:

```
calculate("BAD INPUT");  // This should throw some exciting exception
```

To test that, we use Jasmine like so:

```
expect(function() {
    calculate("BAD INPUT");
}).toThrow();
```

Whether you use an anonymous or named function, you still need to pass a function because Jasmine will call it when running your specs.

Custom Matchers

You can create custom matchers, too! You must add the matcher before every spec in which you want it, you must add it. To do that, we'll be using beforeEach, which is explained in more detail in Chapter 5.

Let's say you want to add a matcher called toBeLarge, which checks if a number is greater than 100. At the very top of a file (or at the top of a describe), you can add the following:

```
beforeEach(function() {
    this.addMatchers({
        toBeLarge: function() {
```

```
            this.message = function() {
                return "Expected " + this.actual + " to be large";
            };
            return this.actual > 100;
        }
    });
});
```

This requires a little bit of knowledge about how Jasmine is put together. Every matcher takes an argument to the expect function, right? expect(200) has 200 as its argument. This argument, in Jasmine, is this.actual when we're defining a new matcher; this.message is a function that, if the matcher *fails*, returns the explanatory output message. Finally, we return a Boolean indicating whether this.actual is large.

Now we can do the following in our specs:

```
expect(5).toBeLarge();        // failure
expect(200).toBeLarge();      // success
expect(12).not.toBeLarge();   // success
```

A more complex matcher might want to introduce this syntax as a replacement for toBeCloseTo:

```
// Expect 6 to be within 2 of 5 (between 3 and 7, inclusive).
expect(6).toBeWithinOf(2, 5);
```

This matcher will take two arguments and is otherwise similar to the previous example:

```
beforeEach(function() {
    this.addMatchers({
        toBeWithinOf: function(distance, base) {
            this.message = function() {
                var lower = base - distance;
                var upper = base + distance;
                return "Expected " + this.actual + " to be between " +
                lower + " and " + upper + " (inclusive)";
            };
            return Math.abs(this.actual - base) <= distance;
        }
    });
});
```

In this example, we're making sure that this.actual is, at most, distance away from base. The message calculates the lower and upper bounds, and the matcher's result is a simple bounds check.

CHAPTER 5

More Jasmine Features

Jasmine has a number of other useful features, which help you write tests that are more advanced.

Before and After

Another useful feature of Jasmine is actually a twofer: `beforeEach` and `afterEach`. They allow you to execute some code—you guessed it—before and after each spec. This can be very useful for factoring out common code or cleaning up variables after tests.

To execute some code *before* every spec, simply put it in a `beforeEach`. Note that you have to scope variables properly in order to have them throughout each spec:

```
describe("employee", function() {
    var employee;    // Note the scoping of this variable.
    beforeEach(function() {
        employee = new Employee;
    });
    it("has a name", function() {
        expect(employee.name).toBeDefined();
    });
    it("has a role", function() {
        expect(employee.role).toBeDefined();
    });
});
```

Similarly, if you'd like to execute something *after* each spec, simply put it in the cleverly named `afterEach`. I use this much less than `beforeEach`, but it's useful when you want to do cleanup, for example:

```
describe("Calculator", function() {
    var calculator = new Calculator;
    afterEach(function() {
        calculator.reset();
```

```
        });
        it("can add two positive integers", function() {
            expect(calculator.add(5, 12)).toEqual(17);
        });
        it("can add two negative integers", function() {
            expect(calculator.add(-5, -12)).toEqual(-17);
        });
    });
```

Nested Suites

As your code gets more complex, you might want to organize your suites into groups, subgroups sub-subgroups, and so on. Jasmine makes it very easy for you to do that by simply nesting the specs.

Put a describe block inside another describe block like this:

```
describe("chat", function() {
    describe("buddy list", function() {
        it("contains a list of users", function() {
            expect(chat.buddyList instanceof Array).toBeTruthy();
            expect(chat.buddyList[0] instanceof chat.User).toBeTruthy();
        });
    });
    describe("messages object", function() {
        it("contains a sender and a body", function() {
            var message = new chat.Message;
            expect(message.body).toEqual("");
            expect(message.sender instanceof chat.User).toBeTruthy();
        });
    });
});
```

To give you an idea of this feature's utility: my most recent project had a group with about 20 subgroups, and each subgroup had about 5 sub-subgroups. Jasmine makes nesting suites very easy indeed!

Skipping Specs and Suites

When you code specs, sometimes you might want to skip a few. Maybe a spec isn't finished; maybe it's too slow; maybe you're just not in the mood to see one red spec in a sea of green ones.

Instead of commenting specs out, just add an x before the word it, and the code will behave as though you had commented the spec out. In the following example, we haven't finished the spec that tests a double rainbow's brightness, so we'll x it out:

```
describe("double rainbow", function() {
    it("is all the way across the sky", function() {
        // This spec will run.
```

```
    });
    xit("is so bright", function() {
        // Because we've x'd this spec out, it won't run.
    });
});
```

Now when you run your specs, you won't see the "double rainbow is so bright" spec at all.

You can also x out entire suites, which will skip all of the specs inside. In this example, none of the Leonardo DiCaprio specs will run:

```
xdescribe("Leonardo DiCaprio", function() {
    it("is not named after Leonardo da Vinci", function() {
        expect("Leonardo DiCaprio").not.toEqual("Leonardo da Vinci");
    });
    it("is in the movie Inception", function() {
        expect(Inception.cast).toContain("Leonardo DiCaprio");
    });
    it("is not in the movie Braveheart", function() {
        expect(Bravehart.cast).not.toContain("Leonardo DiCaprio");
    });
});
```

No specs for poor Leo.

Because all of your specs and suites are defined in functions, you can skip all specs and suites after a certain point in the function with a clever `return`. Because `return` halts a function's execution, you can stop some specs from running, like so:

```
describe("I'm only going to run SOME of these", function() {
  it("will run this spec", function() {});
  it("will run this spec", function() {});
  return;  // This will stop the function from doing anything else.
  it("will not run this spec", function() {});
  it("will not run this spec", function() {});
});
```

This is not a Jasmine feature, but a hack "given to us" from JavaScript. It might be a little unclear to other developers what you're doing, so I'd recommend leaving a comment about the fact that you aren't running some specs.

Matching Class Names

Sometimes you don't care what the value is; you care what *type* it is. To indicate this, use `jasmine.any`. This is a lot like JavaScript's `instanceof` operator, though a bit different with regard to primitive types.

Let's say that we create a function called `rand` that generates a random number. We want to make sure that, no matter what, it returns a number. We don't really care *what* the number is—we just care that it's a number:

```
expect(rand()).toEqual(jasmine.any(Number));
```

Of course, this doesn't just work for numbers. All of these specs succeed:

```
expect("Hello world").toEqual(jasmine.any(String));
expect({}).toEqual(jasmine.any(Object));
expect(new MyObject).toEqual(jasmine.any(MyObject));
```

These are incredibly useful when you want your results to be of a certain type but don't need to be more specific than that.

CHAPTER 6

Spies

As we've learned, Jasmine will let us test if things are working the way we want them to. We want to ability to check if functions have been called, and whether or not they've been called how we want them to be called. We specify how our code should work.

In Jasmine, a *spy* does pretty much what its name implies: it lets you spy on pieces of your program (and in general, the pieces that aren't just variable checks). A little less exciting than James Bond, but still cool spying.

The Basics: Spying on a Function

Spying allows you to replace a part of your program with a spy. A spy can pretend to be a function or an object. When is this useful?

Let's say that you have a class called `Dictionary`. It represents an English dictionary, and can return "hello" and "world":

```
var Dictionary = function() {};
Dictionary.prototype.hello = function() {
    return "hello";
};
Dictionary.prototype.world = function() {
    return "world";
};
```

And now let's say that you have a class called `Person`, which should be able to output "hello world" using `Dictionary` (passed in as an argument). It might work like this:

```
var Person = function() {};
Person.prototype.sayHelloWorld = function(dict) {
    return dict.hello() + " " + dict.world();
};
```

So, to get your `Person` to return "hello world," you'd do something like this:

```
var dictionary = new Dictionary;
var person = new Person;
person.sayHelloWorld(dictionary);  // returns "hello world"
```

You could, in theory, make the sayHelloWorld function return the string literal hello
world, but you don't want that—you want to make sure that your Person consults the
Dictionary.

Spies will help you; you can spy on the dictionary and make sure that it's used. Here's
how to do that:

```
describe("Person", function() {
    it('uses the dictionary to say "hello world"', function() {
        var dictionary = new Dictionary;
        var person = new Person;
        spyOn(dictionary, "hello");  // replace hello function with a spy
        spyOn(dictionary, "world");  // replace world function with another
                                        spy
        person.sayHelloWorld(dictionary);
        expect(dictionary.hello).toHaveBeenCalled();  // not possible without
                                                          first spy
        expect(dictionary.world).toHaveBeenCalled();  // not possible without
                                                          second spy
    });
});
```

Let's go through this, line by line. First, we make our two objects. Then, we'll spyOn the
dictionary's hello and world methods. This basically tells Jasmine to replace dictio
nary.hello and dictionary.world with spies. Very sneaky. Then we call person.say
HelloWorld and make sure that our dictionary's methods were called.

Throwing this through the spec runner should give you positive results; your program
should indeed have called the dictionary methods.

Why is this useful? Say you decide to make your dictionary Spanish instead of English:

```
var Dictionary = function() {};
Dictionary.prototype.hello = function() {
    return "hola";
};
Dictionary.prototype.world = function() {
    return "mundo";
};
```

While sayHelloWorld will return different values, the *exact same spec* will succeed because the dictionary is consulted whether you're using Spanish or English!

OK, maybe that's not all you want. Maybe you want to make sure that +person.
+pass[<phrase role=*keep-together*><literal>sayHelloWorld</literal></phrase>] is
called with a specific dictionary. Jasmine has got your back. Take a look at this example
spec:

```
describe("Person", function() {
    it('uses the dictionary to say "hello world"', function() {
        var dictionary = new Dictionary;
        var person = new Person;
        spyOn(person, "sayHelloWorld");  // replace hello world function with
                                                   a spy
        person.sayHelloWorld(dictionary);
        expect(person.sayHelloWorld).toHaveBeenCalledWith(dictionary);
    });
});
```

As you may be able to read (Jasmine looks a lot like English!), this spy makes sure that sayHelloWorld's argument is dictionary and not some other dictionary object. Run that through Jasmine, and it'll tell you everything is good.

If you want to ensure that something *isn't* called, it's a lot like when you're making sure a variable isn't something: use .not. So, for example, if you want to make sure that a function isn't called with a particular argument, you'd write this:

```
expect(person.sayHelloWorld).not.toHaveBeenCalledWith(dictionary);
```

Calling Through: Making Your Spy Even Smarter

Simply using spyOn makes a spy function that knows whether something's been called.

If you want to spy on a function *and* make sure that it still works, you can *call through*. This makes the spy even sneakier. All you have to do is add andCallThrough to your spyOn call:

```
describe("Person", function() {
    it('uses the dictionary to say "hello world"', function() {
        var dictionary = new Dictionary;
        var person = new Person;
        spyOn(dictionary, "hello");  // replace hello function with a spy
        spyOn(dictionary, "world");  // replace world function with another
                                            spy
        var result = person.sayHelloWorld(dictionary);
        expect(result).toEqual("hello world");  // not possible without
                                                       calling through
        expect(dictionary.hello).toHaveBeenCalled();
        expect(dictionary.world).toHaveBeenCalled();
    });
});
```

This spy function will do everything that the old function did, *and* it will be a good spy and let you see its inner workings.

Making Sure a Spy Returns a Specific Value

You can also make sure that a spy always returns a given value. Let's say that you want the dictionary's `hello` spy to speak French:

```
it("can give a Spanish hello", function() {
    var dictionary = new Dictionary;
    var person = new Person;
    spyOn(dictionary, "hello").andReturn("bonjour");    // note this new piece
    var result = person.sayHelloWorld(dictionary);
    expect(result).toEqual("bonjour world");
});
```

This can be useful if you want to make sure that, despite a changed function, everything else works well. You can also use this to see how your code performs if given bad output. In this example, for instance, `dictionary.hello` might be broken.

Replacing a Function with a Completely Different Spy

Spies can get even crazier. They can call through to a *fake* function, like so:

```
it("can call a fake function", function() {
    var fakeHello = function() {
        alert("I am a spy! Ha ha!");
        return "hello";
    };
    var dictionary = new Dictionary();
    spyOn(dictionary, "hello").andCallFake(fakeHello);
    dictionary.hello();  // does an alert
});
```

This means that you can test your code against, say, a buggy API.

Creating a New Spy Function

In the previous examples, we were building spies that replaced existing functions. It is sometimes useful to create a spy for a function that doesn't yet exist. If you want to, say, give your `Person` a `getName` spy, you can do that by creating a new spy.

Where `spyOn` created a spy by "eating" an existing function, `jasmine.createSpy` doesn't have to. It can make a new one:

```
it("can have a spy function", function() {
    var person = new Person();
    person.getName = jasmine.createSpy("Name spy");
    person.getName();
    expect(person.getName).toHaveBeenCalled();
});
```

Like other spies, spies created with `jasmine.createSpy` can have other methods chained onto them:

```
person.getSecretAgentName = jasmine.createSpy("Name spy").andReturn("James
    Bond");

person.getRealName = jasmine.createSpy("Name spy 2").andCallFake(function() {
        alert("I am also a spy! Ha ha!");
        return "Evan Hahn";
});
```

Creating a New Spy Object

In addition to making a new spy *function*, you can also make a new spy *object*:

```
var tape = jasmine.createSpyObj('tape', ['play', 'pause', 'stop', 'rewind']);
```

It can be used like this:

```
tape.play();
tape.rewind(10);
```

Basically, this creates an object called `tape` that has `play`, `pause`, `stop`, and `rewind` functions. All of those functions are spy functions and act just like the spies we've seen before.

This can be useful for testing whether your code calls an external API.

CHAPTER 7

Using Jasmine with Other Tools

I've demonstrated how to run Jasmine using JavaScript in the browser, but you don't have to do it that way. Jasmine works in a variety of other environments and with other tools.

Jasmine and CoffeeScript

CoffeeScript is a language that compiles to JavaScript, and it's beautiful. It makes coding in JavaScript *much* easier, and it also makes your Jasmine code look better. Using CoffeeScript with Jasmine is a fairly straightforward process, and your specs will look pretty.

If you don't already use CoffeeScript, I'd strongly recommend it. It's easy to learn if you know JavaScript, and it reduces a lot of the headaches that come with JavaScript. There are some people who don't like CoffeeScript, though—it's up to you whether to use it or not.

If you want to give CoffeeScript a try, you can test it out at CoffeesScript.org (*http://coffeescript.org/*), where you'll also find installation instructions and documentation. If you have npm installed, you can install CoffeeScript like so:

```
sudo npm install -g coffee-script
```

If you don't have npm or want to use CoffeeScript in a different way, check the Coffee-Script website for more usage instructions.

One of the things that makes Jasmine specs look nice in CoffeeScript is the language's optional parentheses. The following two lines are equivalent in CoffeeScript:

```
alert("Hello world!")
alert "Hello world!"
```

Because Jasmine's `describe` and `it` are just functions, you can write nice-looking specs that don't have as many brackets and parentheses. You can have specs like this:

```
describe "CoffeeScript Jasmine specs", ->
    it "is beautiful!", ->
        expect("your code is so beautiful").toBeTruthy()
```

Aren't those nice?

Unfortunately, you can't remove the parentheses from the `expect` calls, but you can easily remove them from everything else.

For more about CoffeeScript, take a look at Alex MacCaw's *The Little Book on Coffee-Script* (O'Reilly) (*http://oreil.ly/LB_CoffeeScript*).

Jasmine and Node.js

If you want to use Jasmine to test your Node.js projects, you can! You can use it to test your browser-based projects, too.

Installing jasmine-node on Unix and Linux

First, you need to install the jasmine-node package. Type the following into your terminal:

```
sudo npm install -g jasmine-node
```

The `-g` flag installs jasmine-node on your system globally. If you'd prefer to keep it in a project directory, leave the flag off. This also (probably) means you don't need `sudo` at the front.

Installing jasmine-node on Windows

First, download a ZIP of jasmine-node (*http://bit.ly/WBLMEQ*).

Unpack it and rename the folder as *jasmine-node*. Once you do this, move it into the same directory that you installed `node.exe` into. You should be up and running!

Basic Usage

Now you have jasmine-node installed! Use it as follows:

```
jasmine-node /path/to/project/directory
```

Jasmine-node requires you to put your specs in a directory called *spec* and for the specs in that directory to end with *.spec.js*. You can also put specs in subdirectories of the *spec* directory.

For example, if you have a function like this in *src/test.js*:

```
global.hello = function() {
    return 'world';
};
```

A test spec for that might look like this:

```
// Include what we need to include: this is specific to jasmine-node
require("../src/test.js");

describe("hello", function() {
    it('returns "world"', function() {
        expect(hello()).toEqual("world");
    });
});
```

Other than the `require` calls that you need to make, the specs are just like browser-based Jasmine specs—except for one asynchronous component, that is.

Asynchronous Tests with jasmine-node

Asynchronous tests work the same way as they do in "regular" Jasmine, but there's another syntax that you can use: the done function. This signals to jasmine-node that your spec is, well, done.

Here's an example of how you'd use it:

```
it("does an asynchronous call", function() {
    exampleAsyncCall(function(response) {
        expect(response).toContain("something expected");
        done();
    });
});
```

The done function says to jasmine-node: "Hey, this is a function that deals with asynchronous stuff. Don't call it quits until done is called…unless it takes too long and things time out (after 5 seconds)." You can adjust this timeout value by changing `jasmine.DEFAULT_TIMEOUT_INTERVAL`, like so:

```
// Change default timeout interval to 2 seconds
jasmine.DEFAULT_TIMEOUT_INTERVAL = 2000;
```

jasmine-node and CoffeeScript

If you want to use jasmine-node with CoffeeScript, you can. You'll need to end your filenames with *.spec.coffee* and then run jasmine-node with the `--coffee` flag, like so:

```
jasmine-node /path/to/project/directory --coffee
```

That's all you have to do! Jasmine-node will start picking up *.spec.coffee* files and test them properly.

Jasmine and Ruby on Rails

Jasmine works well with Ruby on Rails, allowing you to test your JavaScript without constantly editing a spec runner HTML file.

The Jasmine documentation recommends one of Ryan Bates's RailsCasts (*http://bit.ly/13Tw7VC*) as a good way to get set up with Jasmine and Rails 3+. I think it is a fantastic resource, so give it a look if you're interested. Or you can follow along here.

Installation

First, you'll need to add Jasmine to your Gemfile, like so:

```
gem "jasmine"
```

Next, let's install it:

```
bundle install
rails generate jasmine:install
```

Usage

Now you're all set up! This process will create a directory called *spec* if you don't already have one. Inside of that, there's a folder called *javascripts*. For this example, let's make a test spec in *spec/javascripts* that just contains this:

```
describe("Jasmine + Rails test", function() {
    it("works", function() {
        expect(true).toBeTruthy();
    });
});
```

Save this as *test.spec.js*.

Now, from any directory, run the following command:

```
rake jasmine
```

After chugging a little bit, Jasmine will tell you that your tests are located at *http://localhost:8888/*. Visit that in your browser, and you'll see the test pass! Now you can change *test.spec.js* to spec out whatever you'd like and go from there.

If you'd like to run your tests in the terminal, you can do that by running `rake jasmine:ci`.

If you have helpers (Jasmine plug-ins, for example), just put them in *spec/javascripts/helpers* and they'll be automatically included.

Jasmine with Non-Rails Ruby

You don't need Rails to use Jasmine with Ruby. First, you need to install the Jasmine gem.

If your project uses Bundler, add the following to your Gemfile:

```
gem "jasmine"
```

If not, run the following commands in the command line:

```
gem install jasmine
```

Once you've installed Jasmine, you can run it like this:

```
jasmine init
rake jasmine:ci
```

You should be up and running!

More Tools

There are countless ways to integrate Jasmine into your project. I've covered only a couple here, but there are *plenty*. There's a section on the Jasmine wiki (*http://bit.ly/XuLbb1*) about using Jasmine with Scala, Java, .NET, and plenty more.

CHAPTER 8

Reference

Jasmine on the Web

- Download Jasmine (*http://github.com/pivotal/jasmine/downloads*)
- Jasmine wiki (*https://github.com/pivotal/jasmine/wiki*)

The Basic Structure of a Suite

```
describe("colors", function() {
    describe("red", function() {
        var red;
        beforeEach(function() {
            red = new Color("red");
        });
        afterEach(function() {
            red = null;
        });
        it("has the correct value", function() {
            expect(red.hex).toEqual("FF0000");
        });
        it("makes orange when mixed with yellow", function() {
            var yellow = new Color("yellow");
            var orange = new Color("orange");
            expect(red.mix(yellow)).toEqual(orange);
        });
    });
});
```

Matchers Reference

- `toEqual` checks for equality, not necessarily the same object.
- `toBe` checks if two objects are the same.
- `toBeTruthy` checks if a value is truthy (not just `true`).
- `toBeFalsy` checks if a value is falsy (not just `false`).
- `toContain` checks if a value is inside another.
- `toBeDefined` checks if a value is defined.
- `toBeUndefined` checks if a value is undefined.
- `toBeNull` checks if a value is null.
- `toBeNaN` checks if a value is NaN.
- `toBeCloseTo` checks decimal proximity.
- `toMatch` checks if a value matches a given regular expression.
- `toThrow` checks if a function throws an error.
- `.not` inverts the meaning of the following matcher.

List of Falsy Values

- `false`
- `0`
- `" "`
- `undefined` (note that the variable `undefined` isn't always undefined!)
- `null`
- `NaN`

Reserved Words in Jasmine

The following are words that you shouldn't use in your code so that you don't cause conflicts with Jasmine:

- `jasmine` (and everything in its namespace)
- `describe`

- it
- expect
- beforeEach
- afterEach
- runs
- waits
- waitsFor
- spyOn
- xdescribe
- xit

These are, of course, in addition to JavaScript's reserved words, which are even more off-limits.

About the Author

Evan Hahn is a JavaScript developer currently enrolled at the University of Michigan. He started coding in BASIC when he was six years old. In high school, he was the webmaster of the online newspaper, where he learned how to develop a website using PHP, mySQL, JavaScript, and jQuery. He most recently worked at UniversityNow, an educational startup in San Francisco.

Colophon

The animal on the cover of *JavaScript Testing for Jasmine* is a phoebe.

The cover image is from Johnson's Natural History. The cover font is Adobe ITC Garamond. The text font is Adobe Minion Pro; the heading font is Adobe Myriad Condensed; and the code font is Dalton Maag's Ubuntu Mono.

Have it your way.

Get even more for your money.

Join the O'Reilly Community, and register the O'Reilly books you own. It's free, and you'll get:

- $4.99 ebook upgrade offer
- 40% upgrade offer on O'Reilly print books
- Membership discounts on books and events
- Free lifetime updates to ebooks and videos
- Multiple ebook formats, DRM FREE
- Participation in the O'Reilly community
- Newsletters
- Account management
- 100% Satisfaction Guarantee

Signing up is easy:

1. **Go to: oreilly.com/go/register**
2. **Create an O'Reilly login.**
3. **Provide your address.**
4. **Register your books.**

Note: English-language books only

To order books online:

oreilly.com/store

For questions about products or an order:

orders@oreilly.com

To sign up to get topic-specific email announcements and/or news about upcoming books, conferences, special offers, and new technologies:

elists@oreilly.com

For technical questions about book content:

booktech@oreilly.com

To submit new book proposals to our editors:

proposals@oreilly.com

O'Reilly books are available in multiple DRM-free ebook formats. For more information:

oreilly.com/ebooks

O'REILLY®

Spreading the knowledge of innovators   oreilly.com

CPSIA information can be obtained at www.ICGtesting.com
Printed in the USA
LVOW03s1342190314

378074LV00028B/625/P